WORKERS
EMERGENCY

SEARCH & RESCUE

by
Jim Ollhoff

VISIT US AT:
WWW.ABDOPUBLISHING.COM

Published by ABDO Publishing Company, PO Box 398166, Minneapolis, MN 55439.
Copyright ©2013 by Abdo Consulting Group, Inc. International copyrights reserved
in all countries. No part of this book may be reproduced in any form without written
permission from the publisher. ABDO & Daughters™ is a trademark and logo of
ABDO Publishing Company.

Printed in the United States of America, North Mankato, Minnesota.
032012
092012

PRINTED ON RECYCLED PAPER

Editor: John Hamilton
Graphic Design: Sue Hamilton
Cover Design: Neil Klinepier
Cover Photo: iStockphoto
Interior Photos and Illustrations: Adventure Medical-pg 8; AP-pgs 3, 11, 15, 20 &
21; Corbis-pg 5; FEMA/Jocelyn Augustino-pgs 1, 9, 17, 29 & Sidebars; FEMA/Butch
Kinerney-pgs 18, 19 & 32; FEMA/Marvin Nauman-pg 25; FEMA/Andrea Booher-pg 27;
FEMA/Adam DuBrowa-pg 28; Getty-pg 26; iStockphoto-pg 7; Thinkstock-pgs 6, 10, 14,
22 & 23; United States Coast Guard-pg 13 and Sidebar on pgs 12 & 30.

ABDO Booklinks

To learn more about Emergency Workers, visit ABDO Publishing Company online.
Web sites about Emergency Workers are featured on our Book Links pages. These links
are routinely monitored and updated to provide the most current information available.
Web site: www.abdopublishing.com

Library of Congress Cataloging-in-Publication Data

Ollhoff, Jim, 1959-
  Search & rescue / Jim Ollhoff.
      p. cm. -- (Emergency Workers)
  Audience: 10-14
  Includes index.
  ISBN 978-1-61783-516-2
  1. Search and rescue operations--Juvenile literature. 2. Volunteer workers in search and
rescue operations--Juvenile literature. I. Title. II. Title: Search and rescue.
  TL553.8.O456 2013
  363.1'081--dc23
                                    2012005331

TABLE OF CONTENTS

SEARCH & RESCUE

Two hikers, high in the mountains, have not been heard from for days. Fear grows that they are lost or injured. A search-and-rescue team jumps into action. Team members scan large areas with a helicopter. They study the area where the hikers were last seen. They look for clues to where the hikers might have strayed.

This is the world of search-and-rescue technicians. Many of them are volunteers. Many are on call, 24 hours a day, seven days a week. All are dedicated professionals, willing to risk everything to find victims who are trapped, lost, or injured.

Performing a search might be as simple as walking through a field, looking for someone who is lost or injured. But searching is often much more difficult. It might mean hiking through dangerous mountain terrain. It might mean crossing rushing water. It might mean looking in places that contain toxic materials. Search-and-rescue members sometimes have to lower themselves off cliffs or leap into the ocean to perform rescues. It can be a very dangerous job, but also very rewarding.

Search-and-rescue technicians stabilize an injured climber and then study the area to find the safest way to transport the victim off the mountain.

SEARCH & RESCUE TRAINING

Training is very important for search-and-rescue team members. If they are not trained well, they may perform searches poorly or get lost themselves. Untrained people can get hurt and make a rescue situation even worse.

Search-and-rescue technicians are trained to use a compass, map, and GPS.

One of the most useful types of training is first aid. When victims become lost, it is often because they are injured. Search-and-rescue personnel can treat life-threatening injuries until medical help arrives.

Search-and-rescue technicians are trained in search techniques, the use of maps, and how to read a compass and operate a GPS. There are many training courses available. Special training is also available for specific regions or states.

Many firefighters and police receive search-and-rescue training, since they are often the first to arrive at accident scenes. Sometimes victims are lost or trapped in places containing hazardous materials (hazmat). To prepare for this situation, hazmat technicians often receive search-and-rescue training.

Firefighters practice their search-and-rescue training, performing CPR on a victim.

SEARCH & RESCUE GEAR

An example of a portable first-aid kit.

The equipment used by search-and-rescue teams depends on the areas being searched. Sometimes a good pair of shoes and heavy gloves are all that are needed. If a search takes place in an urban area after a disaster, teams may need hardhats, flashlights, safety goggles, and dust masks. A well-stocked first-aid kit can help the injured.

If a search takes place far out in a forest or on a mountainside, teams may need multi-purpose knives, signal flares, and extra food and water. A large tarp helps keep things dry and also functions as a makeshift shelter or stretcher. Waterproof boots and clothing are essential in wet weather or in wetlands. Cell phones or two-way communication devices are a must. GPS systems can help search-and-rescue workers know where they are and where they need to go.

Sometimes search-and-rescue teams wear uniforms. The sight of the uniform can help victims remain calm, because they know that help has arrived.

Members of the FEMA Urban Search and Rescue task force prepare their gear prior to going into areas impacted by Hurricane Katrina in 2005.

GROUND SEARCH & RESCUE

Search-and-rescue teams are trained for the terrains they face. If they live in a city at the base of a mountain, they are trained for mountain search and rescue. If they live by the ocean, they are trained for sea rescue.

Most areas in North America have ground search-and-rescue teams. A team can quickly come together to find someone who is reported lost. It may be a missing child. It may be a lost elderly person with Alzheimer's, a disease that robs people of their memory.

Teams of people, often directed by local fire or sheriff's departments, will gather to perform the search and rescue. These people have special training in search and rescue, including learning how people who are lost behave. They learn how to look for clues. They learn how to navigate so that they don't get lost themselves. They also learn first aid and how to rescue someone once they are found.

A search-and-rescue team gathers to look for a lost hiker in New Hampshire. The man, separated from his friends during unexpectedly high winds and snow, was found and brought home safely.

AIR-SEA SEARCH & RESCUE

Air-sea search and rescue is any rescue where people are in the water. It might include a boat that has capsized, or a plane that has crashed into the ocean. Air-sea rescue teams can use boats, helicopters, planes, and even submarines to find and assist lost or injured people.

Helicopters are the most effective at air-sea rescue. They can hover over someone in the water, and they can fly during stormy weather conditions. Sometimes, people called rescue swimmers leap into the water to rescue victims. Rescue swimmers have to be courageous, excellent swimmers, and knowledgeable about first aid.

In cities or areas with large lakes or rivers, many search-and-rescue teams are available at a moment's notice. They often work with local fire, police, or sheriff's departments.

The United States Coast Guard is active in air-sea search and rescue. Many boats and planes today have emergency beacons that broadcast their location in an emergency. These beacons have saved many lives, since the Coast Guard and other rescuers can immediately find the ships and planes in distress.

United States Coast Guard personnel practice an air-sea rescue operation.

MOUNTAIN SEARCH & RESCUE

Search and rescue in mountainous areas presents

Unexpected winds can cause people to become disoriented in the snow.

lots of challenges. Rescuers often have difficulty getting to isolated areas. Even if injured or lost climbers can communicate with rescuers, they may not know their exact location. Climbers can get disoriented or further lost, or fall into crevices. They can get injured quickly. Climbers can get dehydrated or contract hypothermia, a condition caused by cold temperatures. Fog can hinder search and rescue, and storms and bad weather can happen quickly in mountainous areas.

Whether volunteers or paid professionals, rescue teams spring into action when someone is reported lost or injured. In large, well-traveled national parks, it is more likely that paid rescue teams are available.

Helicopters are often used to search for lost and injured hikers. Nothing is better than a helicopter to get to an isolated location quickly, pick up victims, and transport them to safety. However, rescuers have to be careful with helicopters. Unexpected wind gusts can make flying helicopters very hazardous.

Life Flight, a rescue service, hoists an injured hiker and a paramedic off Mount Olympus, near Salt Lake City, Utah. A total of four injured hikers and rescue personnel waited on the mountain overnight until morning when it was safe for the helicopter to come in.

URBAN SEARCH & RESCUE

Urban search and rescue is usually used in cities that have suffered through some kind of disaster. It might be a tornado that has caused damage in a large area. A hurricane or flood might have swept through. An earthquake or explosion may have caused buildings to collapse. In each of these situations, urban search-and-rescue teams go to work.

Search-and-rescue workers first assess the damage. What exactly happened? Has one building collapsed, or many? Is it likely that many people are trapped, or only a few? Are there hazardous materials leaking? Are there downed power lines or other things that could be risky for the victims or rescuers?

Figuring out the situation is sometimes harder than it seems. If there was an explosion, for example, everyone is frightened. Was it a terrorist attack or leaking natural gas? Will there be another explosion? Many people are injured, and everyone will have a different story of what happened. Police and firefighters are trying to help. There are so many different needs that it is sometimes difficult to see exactly what is going on. But once police and firefighters have made sure it is safe for rescuers, the search-and-rescue teams go to work.

An urban search-and-rescue team brings flood victims to dry land in New Orleans, Louisiana, in 2005.

Rescue teams fan out over the city, searching for people who are trapped and injured. When they enter a damaged building, they make a slash mark on the doorway with paint. This tells others that there is a rescue team inside, and prevents other teams from re-searching the building and wasting time. It can also help if the building collapses and traps the rescuers. Other rescuers will then know that a rescue team is still inside.

When the rescue team exits the building, they paint another slash mark, making an "X." This shows that the building has been searched. The team may also write a message telling if there are dangerous hazards inside or if there are dead bodies present. In a search and rescue operation, the teams will look for living people first, who may need immediate medical attention. When all the injured are rescued, they will then go back to retrieve the dead bodies.

Once a building is checked for survivors, it is marked with an "X." This lets other rescuers know that the building has been searched.

A rescue team prepares to enter and search for injured people in a building damaged by Hurricane Ivan in Orange Beach, Alabama, in 2004.

SEARCH & RESCUE WITH DOGS

Trained dogs are very useful for search and rescue teams. One trained dog can work better than a dozen humans. A dog's sense of smell is very sensitive. It can learn a person's scent, and then find the person using its nose. Since a lot of searching is done at night, dogs are especially useful. Dogs can sniff for scents when humans can't see in the dark.

Dogs have to be specially trained for search-and-rescue work. Training can take up to two years. A trained dog will remain a search-and-rescue dog for its whole life.

Dogs, and their trained owners, can also get training and certification in very specific areas. Some dogs are trained to find people in avalanches, or in the buried rubble of collapsed buildings. Some dogs are trained and certified to find people who are lost in forests. Other dogs are trained to find dead bodies on land or in water.

A rescue dog trains to find a person buried in an avalanche.

A trained owner and dog work to find a dead body in a stream.

INTERVIEW WITH A SEARCH & RESCUE WORKER

Search-and-rescue team member Amee Pribyl is a 20-year veteran of police work. She has served in patrol, forensics, search and rescue, judicial security, investigations, and has extensive training in many other law enforcement areas.

Q: How did you get interested in becoming a member of a search-and-rescue team?

Amee: I enjoy helping people, and I love working outdoors. Being a member of a search-and-rescue team means I can do both—help people and work outdoors.

Q: What is an average day like?

Amee: When the team gets called out, I respond to the location with the necessary gear for that type of search-and-rescue operation. Sometimes the team needs to search a wooded area for a missing child, or a cornfield for a gun used in a crime, and sometimes the team needs to search in the water.

Rescue personnel use tools to get to a victim trapped in a car.

Q: What is your most memorable experience as a search-and-rescue team member?

Amee: It was a beautiful sunny day, and I was called to a cabin by a lake. A little girl had been missing for about an hour and the family was frantic and believed she had gone down to the lake. As we were about to jump into the water to search in the lake, a neighbor yelled that he had found her. She had walked over a half-mile (.8 km) through a thick, wooded area.

Q: What is the best part about being a member of a search-and-rescue team?

Amee: The best part about being a member of a search-and-rescue team is that every situation is different and a new adventure. Sometimes the team can be searching a remote park in a snowstorm, and the next day the team could be searching a flooded river.

Q: What advice would you give to kids who want to be members of a search-and-rescue team?

Amee: If you enjoy working outdoors and are looking for challenging adventures, then you can also be a member of a search-and-rescue team. Most law enforcement agencies have a volunteer search-and-rescue unit. When you're old enough, you can contact your local sheriff's department to see if you can attend a training day. Then you can see what it's like to be a member of the local search-and-rescue team.

A rescue team searches for people stranded in a flood in Kingfisher, Oklahoma, in August 2007. Search-and-rescue teams may search for flood victims in a city one day, and the next day search a forest for a lost child.

FEMA

FEMA

FEDERAL EMERGENCY MANAGEMENT AGENCY
WASHINGTON

One of the important agencies of the government is the Federal Emergency Management Agency (FEMA). This organization is the government's way of helping communities that have suffered through some kind of a disaster.

Disasters often strike very large areas, such as when a hurricane damages communities across many states. This kind of disaster overwhelms local city and state authorities. When a state governor and the president of the United States declare that a place is "a disaster area," then FEMA moves quickly to help.

There are many kinds of disasters, and FEMA trains to be prepared for them all. If there is citywide damage with many people missing, such as after an earthquake, FEMA might send in its Urban Search and Rescue teams. If many people are left homeless, FEMA may set up temporary shelters for them. If many people are injured, FEMA could bring in doctors and EMTs.

In 1979, the government formed FEMA to be responsible for emergency disaster planning and relief. In its early days, the agency was praised for its ability to move quickly and make decisions to help disaster victims.

The Federal Emergency Management Agency (FEMA) assists people after an area has been declared a "disaster area." This could include bringing in search-and-rescue teams, as well as setting up temporary shelters with food and water and medical assistance.

27

However, FEMA didn't always perform well. In 2003, FEMA became an agency within the United States Department of Homeland Security. The first big test of this new relationship happened in 2005 when Hurricane Katrina struck New Orleans, Louisiana, and the Gulf Coast. The storm was the most devastating natural disaster in United States history, killing hundreds of people and causing horrific damage.

FEMA managers waited for permission to act from the managers at the Department of Homeland Security. Simple decisions took days to make. FEMA's painfully slow response made the situation much worse.

In 2006, after a long investigation, Congress reorganized FEMA and its relationship with the Department of Homeland Security in hopes that FEMA could better carry out its duties.

Today, FEMA spends its resources on disaster relief, but it also helps communities prepare for disasters. The agency also trains groups of people for urban search and rescue, or to create emergency housing, or even to handle radioactive nuclear waste spills. Despite the criticisms of the agency, FEMA remains the government's important first responder.

Sandy, a member of the California Urban Search and Rescue Team, is on hand at a FEMA Safety Preparedness Expo.

While there were many problems with FEMA's response after Hurricane Katrina, Urban Search and Rescue members helped thousands of people in Louisiana and on the Gulf Coast.

GLOSSARY

COAST GUARD, UNITED STATES

A part of the United States military created in 1967. Coast Guard forces are responsible for guarding America's coast, preventing smuggling, as well as helping people in danger on America's coast.

DEHYDRATE

Extreme loss of water from the body, often because no water is available, or because of an illness.

DEPARTMENT OF HOMELAND SECURITY

A United States government agency whose members are given the task of protecting America. This includes protecting the United States and its territories from terrorist attacks, as well as helping during times of natural disasters, such as floods, tornadoes, hurricanes, and earthquakes.

DISORIENTED

Confused and lost. In poor weather conditions, such as in heavy snow, rain, or winds, people may lose their sense of direction and become lost.

EMERGENCY MEDICAL TECHNICIAN (EMT)

A person trained to provide emergency care to victims before and while being taken to a hospital.

FEMA (FEDERAL EMERGENCY MANAGEMENT AGENCY)

An agency created in 1979 by the United States government to assist people during times of disaster. Today it is a part of the United States government's Department of Homeland Security.

FORENSICS

Forensics is the use of science and technology to investigate a crime and provide facts in a court of law.

GPS (GLOBAL POSITIONING SYSTEM)

A system used to pinpoint where a person is located based on satellite tracking.

HAZMAT

Hazmat is short for "hazardous materials." People who are hazmat technicians respond to toxic spills or leaks of dangerous chemicals.

HYPOTHERMIA

A condition in which a person has an abnormally low body temperature. This is usually caused by long exposure to cold weather or cold water. If the body cannot be warmed, a person risks death.

TOXIC

Poisonous. A substance that may cause death.

URBAN SEARCH AND RESCUE

The search and rescue of people who are trapped in damaged buildings and cities, such as after an earthquake.

INDEX